Mystics Recourse

Mayapple Arts

Frederick, Maryland

But today well lived
makes every yesterday a dream of happiness,
and every tomorrow a vision of hope.
Look well therefore to this day!
Such is the salutation of the dawn.

~ Sanskrit poem

For my mother and father, who instilled in me a great love for the English language, and who conceded to me the creative freedom I have had in my life. In retrospect, it was worth the challenges.

May people everywhere express greater compassion for the sick, for the healthy often do not know what a great gift they have been given simply in being well.

This book is dedicated to all cancer survivors, and to the memory of those who have not survived this costly disease's ravages. There are too many of us. Though we live on, we are changed forever.

Mystics Recourse
A Poetic Journey
Robert Strasser

Table of Contents

Introduction

Without poetry, there would be less color in the world. The artistic side of human expression would be missing critical voices. Poets, among the oldest of scholars and intellects, often performed together with musicians. Sometimes these balladeers had skills in both areas, making them one-man acts. Bands today are typically poets mixed together with musicians. They are highly valued. They still comment around the edges or beyond the edges of social norms today, risking consequences for the chance to freely express themselves. This is something that makes them unique, artists in their own right, worthy of praise.

Poets have articulated the need to examine, celebrate, authenticate, and protest. Change has come to society in various ways because of them, and in spite of them. Technology probably being the fastest of all changes, music keeps up with it currently. It is sometimes terrifying how quickly we proceed. Artificial intelligence can write poetry. It's pretty good. But it lacks human characteristics in more subtle ways if examined closely. It also writes songs. Who knows what it won't do without proper training and constraints. Certainly, we cannot let it take over too much, or we lose our individuality and become subservient.

Original voices are under a certain amount of threat from AI. I am one who believes it won't take over completely. Will it

1

always serve, never rule? We will see. I may be wrong. Our planet speeds toward automation and abstraction from nature, while conformity takes so many along for the ride that it's hard to imagine what defines original anymore. To me, dependence on artificial intelligence, and its limitations in some areas, is more scary than it is reassuring. I personally think that AI won't stop evolving. I don't know where I will be in the matrix, but we must live alongside of this harbinger of the brave new world we now are entering.

True connection with the natural world, that fundamentally important source of renewal, has become scarcer for the majority. People mostly live in urban centers, where they don't get enough forest time, enough sunlight, enough true peace.

May these poems provide grist for the mill and food for thought. May nature play a part. And may they also give deeper nourishment to that intangible thing called the soul, called love.

This book was written over several years, and under very different kinds of circumstances. The lyrical poems tend to be older, the free verse more recent. Many others are from the period when I had cancer (2021 – 2023). I even wrote a few after editing had begun and I was over the worst of my treatment in 2024-5.

Whatever their source, all filled the need for creative expression in me. Simultaneously, they now speak to a larger audience. Through reaching readers, poetry realizes its truest purpose. I hope they find something in you that needs them, that they speak to you personally, give you something fresh to work with.

For at least ten years, I was given to journaling. There was no TV. Much was self-reflective, and on spiritual matters. There was a lot of growth, especially in spiritual directions. I hungered for more. Poems were occasional. The writing process held meaning and helped to reconcile conflicts and absences I felt in modern life, but it was almost too personal to share with others. This, and studio arts, kept me sane. Creativity gave me places to channel energy for ten years when I lived on a busy corner in town and often lamented the fact. I matured, went thru crisis, and turned to poetry more.

In 2020, I was in transition, on my way West to start a new chapter in life. I didn't get far. First, COVID struck. I was forced into winter quarters in the mountains on short notice. During that isolating winter, I decided to write more seriously to pass the time and work for some new goals. Covid wasn't going away.

Just as I got going, in March of 2021, came a diagnosis of stage 4, non-Hodgkins T-cell lymphoma. Things didn't look good at all. I was 56. Maybe there were not going to be too many tomorrows?

For a month in the hospital, my life hung in the balance, while we waited for a definitive diagnosis, and treatment for the cancer. Fortunately, the rare lymphoma I had did in fact have a treatment, though it was rough.

Tenuousness defined chemotherapy. Four and a half months and my white blood cell count was close to zero. I could take no more. I survived. But remission lasted only six months, when I had to have more chemo, followed closely by whole body radiation, and finally a stem cell transplant from my 26-year-old nephew. This time it worked, but life hasn't been completely the same since. And it never will be.

Between the back surgery I had to stabilize my spine, and undergoing chemotherapy itself, I was in no position to do much except survive. This survival mode went on in one form or another for years.

I had severely high blood glucose and then diabetes for six months, all due to very high prednisone doses, and had to be hospitalized for several days. I had dangerous levels of anemia, and again was hospitalized for four days. I gave myself insulin injections for six months. Getting better, getting worse, getting better again, falling behind - It seemed endless. I was dying inside, where it hurt most. I felt spun around and tossed out onto the streets of a cold, and indifferent world.

Now, in year 4, I am much better, but some days still feel like I'm just barely functional, or would prefer to stay in bed. I ignore the pain that never goes away. On other days, I feel exalted just to be alive and summoned to new heights of creativity. Somehow it comes out poetry.

The back pain occurs daily. It's very difficult sometimes, more bearable at others. I sense time is short, like a subtle shadow in my wake, reminding me of mortality. I have befriended pain. But I can ignore pain only so long before it wears me down heavily. Occasionally, I breakdown and need a place just to rest, sleep, regroup. It takes a lot of effort. I wonder if it will end. I reach for the sky. I strive for normal. It's a wild ride.

Cancer survivors carry fear of what most others don't have to notice. The thought of resurgence is terrifying. Treatment is straight forward enough, though things are lost that cannot be retrieved. Neuropathy, fatigue, and isolation are a toxic cocktail. Chemotherapy cannot be repeated more than a few times. Then its hospice.

I can't return to who I was. I know that to be true without a doubt. My sister says I am a special person. I appreciate that, but am I really approaching a new norm or steadily in decline?

Normal is not the word I would choose. Its uncharted territory I now entered. It is too soon to tell with assurance what will happen to me, but I am hopeful things will return to greater balance soon. I think I can, as long as I keep on fighting cancer, stay balanced.

I slow down, and appreciate more and more. I do not know how long I have, but don't dwell on the thought too long. We should all live like this. Death is peace. Easy. The final rest. But I prefer the idea of doing so at a ripe old age. And while people hurry about life, fitting it all in on limited time, I depart the beaten path. Many cannot. I am lucky and very unlucky at one and the same time. In nature and frequent solitude I find my reserve, and my resolve. But it is a life apart, a different way of being in ways many people don't understand.

It's a paradox, this life. The only constant is change itself. We fail, and if progress has anything with it, don't make the same mistakes twice. You fail many times before you finally see the biggest picture, understand how society functions and doesn't function, and how not to fail, yet you will probably fail again at times, in some way. Its only human.

I have been transformed. I can think more carefully, when it doesn't hurt too much. I am lighter, freer, still am agitated, yet endure. Edges of experience define my life. And my writing has become so very meaningful. No one can take that away. It's very liberating, and keeps things very interesting.

At times I don't know what to say that hasn't already been said. So, I say nothing. Or I feel unheard, broken in a world that casts broken things aside. Its maddening.

I suffer, and rejoice, silently. Cancer inspires a lot of fear, so people avoid it or ease into it more than I had the luxury of doing. I have looked at death right in the face and said not yet, there are many things I still want to do with this life.

Interestingly, cancer survivors themselves have the least aversion to hearing about my traumas. They understand. But ultimately, we face cancer alone while others assist or watch. I was helpless in the hospital, depending upon nurses for everything while doctors hurried to find a cure. Then I became more self-reliant, people helped me less and viewed me a cured. But there is no total cure for cancer, fear persists like that dark shadow.

More often, it's a question of what is to be done with the aftermath. I don't think society knows any better than I do what to do with all the cancer patients, and there are too few resources to go around. How do we fit in? Who will love us? What to do with all the doctor bills, medical appointments, the inability to work like I used to. The latter question is one of my biggest burdens. Money.

My reaction has generally been to do what brings me joy, to focus, and to reach out for help now that I am much improved. I endure and live with a foot in each of two worlds, preferring to live and let live.

I've been through so much in so little time. I'm still playing catch-up. I am very grateful to be alive. At times I feel quite alone. We live in an imperfect society. People get left behind. I hope I don't.

Worse yet is that I believe a doctor gave me cancer. I did a lot of research to learn this. Medicine prescribed for autoimmune disease risks lymphoma, and the longer you take it, the higher the risk. My gastroenterologist should have recommended another medicine, but didn't. So, I took it for too long. He takes little responsibility for nearly killing me, leaving the wreckage of my life for me to take care of. Doctors hide behind carefully crafted laws that protect them. Some protections have good reason, but some are terrible. This gives them cause to cut corners, be negligent while nobody knows the difference.

The **third leading cause of death in the US is medical mistake**. I am one of the survivors. Heartbroken and rather discouraged, I paid all the price, completely and profoundly, yet they ignore the question of guilt because they pass out medication easily and don't have to think about the questions too much. If it's approved for use in humans, it becomes the standard of care. One size does not fit all, though. The battle for better organization persists.

That is where writing becomes especially valuable. I consider deeply, because I must. It's the direction that makes sense. Anything else pales in comparison. I have been given an ironic gift. It came on fast after years of slow growth, including several years lost mostly to cancer and its aftermath.

These poems are about places that spoke to me, in illness and in recovery, with and without active cancer. A few came from the need to think more about the environment, what we are doing, and not doing, to care for a precious thing.

Others are about simple things, like friendship and love, small rites of passage, imaginings, reminders of fun times had under better circumstances.

Still others come from more profound or slightly taboo places, commenting on stages of life, passages, or the need to muster the strength to continue when deeper states of fatalism or depression take hold. It's all very vivid, potent, and sincere.

Nevertheless, I hope you find pleasure in, and share the joy and pain, irony and paradox, that I express in words. Pain is an inevitable part of life for all of us. We must rise above it with all the strength we can summon.

We are all on a journey through life, simultaneously looking back and forward, while trying to remain in the present. This much is possible if we try.

If you seek Enlightenment, it's available on Earth, in your lifetime. Practice humility, be a good person; Accept new ideas, and research them compared to talk on the street; Do charity.

Fly up into wonder, look around, and believe you can fly higher, but watch for your safety. What some call love, or Love, others call Humanism, still others the Truth, the Way, or Reality. What a sad world it would be if you didn't have cause to feel appreciation, to express it. Give for the sheer pleasure in giving. While you have wings to fly upon, the world is yours to explore. We are for the most part gifted with long lives. Enjoy.

"Illusion makes the world close in.

Enlightenment opens it on every side."

~ Buddhist saying

The Color of Music

Wildflowers dance
perfectly
each its own
being
one whole note
in the brilliant cacophony
of music
the breezes make
of their colors.

Dreamers Dream

I sometimes feel
like a moth to the flame
instinctively, blindly drawn
to the dance,
the flickering allure,
of love's bright candle burning.

Flowers are for love,
in sun or in moonlight,
and inspire the dreams
dreamers dream.

While I dream of flowers,
and you dream of twilight,
we both hold lovers esteemed.

The power that renews them,
like a well-tuned harp,
plucked gently
and ever so slow.

Slow like the morning,
gentle like the evening,
softly lingering,
until candles burn low.

Clear comes the music,
and with it the love,
in concert with heart's desire.

Ever so gently,

ever

so

slowly,

the moth isn't blind to allure.

Just Once

We had our laughs
with each other,
for each other
at each other, even.
But just a little bit,
pure fun,
backed up with caring,
your signature style.
You caught me
more than a few times,
with that dry humor.
Too dry, often,
for my literal mind.

This was that kind of afternoon,
but balanced just right.
Luminous met the quiet
in unspoken ways,
in creative collaboration.

We thought nothing of it at the time.
Imaginings, simple magic, playing,
and no place we had to be.
That long afternoon
spent in quiet absorption,
working with color and line,
shape and arc.

A composition for two
as the sun shone down
angling, silent and bright
from the clerestory.

Our work our play,
 sitting there on an old,
 worn wooden floor.

Happy to be friends
with nowhere to go
in a place apart,
a room with no limits
just for a while.
 our time our own.

Finding Something New

In my favorite book of poems
many folded corners
mark the pages
containing the words
that have inspired me.

I am lost
trying to find one
that I have not read
a hundred ways.

It is said
that to be truly seen,
the eyes of the beholder
and those of the beholden
must converge at once,
and for a long time.

I would like for this book
to be like that saying,
so much
do I love
to read the words
that mystify
like the sky.

Poem For Rose

What is God
but love
at the heart of infinity?

Living this way
might just be
the best thing.

It's a form of being fully alive,
Awake without bluster or laziness
to obscure the view.

Like some tousled, ebullient bird,
feathers washed with the same dust
to which she will someday return,
I give no thought
to what others think.
I am alive, and that is enough.

All the world shimmers,
thrilled to be
so very many,
and yet one small part
of a whole universe
sparkling infinitely
and united
by Light.

Expect To Fly

When we are at our best,
the last thing we need
is the pain of others.

And when we are at our worst,
the first thing we need
is the honest compassion
that others can share.

What you are seeking is there in the details.

If it is within your grasp,
accept it gratefully.
If not, reach out expectantly.
If no-one responds, let it go.
It will come back if it is meant to be.

What is possession?
Holding onto something
that has a will all its own
is risky business.

Open your fist
so that the doves may transform
all that does not serve light
as they fly to their freedom.

Nothing Without Light

Expressing itself endlessly,
life becomes life becomes life,
again and again,
ad infinitum.

The eternal renewal,
yesterday and tomorrow,
always becoming, almost forever.

Repeating what has been repeated since the beginning.
DNA tells and it reads, it translates and it expresses.
It rests and it wakes,
changing slowly,
never truly dying.

This compound intertwining is so much more
than information busy repeating itself.
We exist, we work, we know.
But we also love.

Equilibrium, stasis, change,
balancing and letting go.
Ours is the dance
of all living things.

Threads weave a shared reality.
Everyone has a part in the way forward,
our shared sacred trust.

Life in the Open

I am not sure
what is more beautiful,
the pulsing ocean
or the endless sky,
a butterfly's wing,
or the true eyes of love.

Water flowing downhill
must sometimes cross great distances,
its purpose simple, enduring,
before it reaches the sea.

Stars, compellingly fierce,
distant and secure,
express light
that travels forever.

How do they shine so constantly in their brilliance?
The scale is unfathomable.

Philosophers and scientists
open doors
for the sake of knowing.

They learn as much as they can,
then they must decide what to believe.

Some have gotten lost
without heart,
dissecting knowledge
until nothing is left
but more of the same.

This goes on and on forever.
There's no end to it
unless we break the spell.

A true seeker opens doors for the sake of seeing,
and walks through to another place,
only to see
what lies
inside of Light
is only
more
Light.

Bright, Bright

Bright, bright
the forest bright,
come and play with me.

Bright, bright
the fields of light,
come this way and see
that this will always be
come, and stay with me.

Sunrise

Sunrise,
mid-day,
sunset.

Light filters
through canopy leaves,
it's dappled grace
patterning a mosaic
across the forest floor.

This slow dance
lasts all day,
each moment
an unfolding eternity.

Epiphany

Before,
I sought pleasure
in pure temptation –
chocolate, caresses, wine.

Now the emptiness
gives my deepest yearnings
space to sing.

Morning Glory

This blue flower that you hold
feels like an invitation
to tune my guitar and play
songs of spirit,
or something completely new.

I am swept halfway to God
in a moment's ease,
left with no choice
but to sing.

Heart of Being

I have no certainty
about what is to come.
But in this place, I am not afraid.

The clarity I feel now will be there, too, when needed.
I still seek sincerely and listen.

I am open.

In the future,
the knowledge which I have gained,
lost, and gained again
on paths to wisdom
will guide me.

People follow and lead,
react and fret,
control, succeed, and fail.
All in endless struggles
with limited time.
It's a perpetual game.
So, we are all Sisyphus until we learn to free ourselves.

Because what the world does is to turn,
and in turning,
it turns us.

Maelstrom or eddy,
it is fluid reality
that we love
and sometimes fear.

But of rivers running downhill,
or the seemingly eternal pulse of the seas,
I have a feeling of ease so great,
no fear can erase.

The gift of life is everything.
True sustenance we must weave into our tableau daily,
and be open to when it's not clear.

Undoing is inevitable
in the theatre of eternity.
We are all passengers and pilots,
makers and destroyers.

When you find your peace,
feel thanks
and stay inside.
The heart of being true to yourself
starts and ends
with love.

The Time Is Right

Without a doubt
fire smolders
until the time is right.

You too
will exist
as a semblance
of what can be
if only, if only, **if only.**

But there is only now,
only these truths,
only this time.
It can be maddening.

Small growth pains
turn into grist
for the mill of your being
again and again.

The future is patient
beyond all measures.
Until enough time passes,
weeks into months,
entire seasons ripening.
then at last it happens.

You've given something you had
for everything that still can be.

Queen Anne's Does

she will always belong in my memory
like family, like a sister I had known half a lifetime
but had only gotten to know well
for just a while

what I remember most
about Rebecca
is her smile
how it opened naturally
came easily
on an early summer afternoon
sunshine and mirth
pure gold

and I can hear her voice, too
across the years
almost bashfully
explaining the rules
and demonstrating
to my then perplexed mind
how to play

made up, like all good things
for simple fun
guessing words as we drove
easily along a country road

landscapes, signs, names of things within view
all were fair game

I preferred the view
just a little more
but didn't say

but fun was inviting me
so, I had an ear for the game

Queen Anne's does, she spoke
Mickey guessed something in reply, was wrong

two guesses to go
Queen Anne's does, she again quipped
a humorous tone entering her voice

again, he guessed
again, was wrong
he was watching the road, after all

Queen Anne's does
she offered him his third
and final chance

Scattergood, he guessed
right, she affirmed
you got it

it was that easy, she explained

I followed, at least I thought I did
but was admittedly lost
part of my attention was still on the view
rolling corn fields and pasture
nice in their own right

I straightened
looked out the window

try, she said
and so, I did

I got it wrong, of course
I didn't even know all the rules yet
and a little part of my attention
of necessity
was still on the view

but I tried again
and still got it wrong
actually, there weren't that many rules

THEN she explained:
double letters once
you score one
double letters twice

you score double

oh, I said
that's a little hard
and it was
simple, and a little bit hard
especially for those who were only half listening

it took practice, to be sure
I didn't get much time to practice
not that time
during the few minutes
we had remaining
before returning to Scattergood *
people dispersing into the crowd
gathering for goodbye

I will always remember that time, though
simple and easy
special
like a sweet summer afternoon
like her smile

*Scattergood is a small Quaker boarding and day school near Iowa City, Iowa, that offers a farm-based, experiential education. Rebecca and I attended together in 1980. The scene described in the poem was at a 25th class reunion. Rebecca was lost to cancer a few years later.

The Gold In Your I

When the crucible that holds your molten pain
stops becoming Me,
true metamorphosis begins.

No longer molten,
gold reveals its brightness and strength,
yet remains soft.

Don't forget this - You are mostly water.
Vanish into this liquid life
and reappear when you have drunk enough ease.
Swim for the pure joy in it.

This is existence:
Before the paint dries on the canvas of your mind,
your own original moment
is soft like the sea,
then becomes opaque,
and then
solid.

The great moon moves with our whole earth
in an eternal dance
that dwarfs our little selves.
Such immensity
is to be deeply admired.

35

Nothing stays the same.

Just love everything,
and in the complex reality of being,
and remember:

In Love means believing,
and everything has its truth.

Your path goes on
almost forever,
until others
pick up the pieces,
carrying the essence
forward again.

Lark

Lark,
how do you respond
with dust close to your eyes
clouding your freedom,
tears blocked
by layers fast forming
surrounding the edges
of your clever
sensitive eyes?

All who look upon you
can see grief building.
All who can feel,
feel for you.

Your pain –
it is ours, too.
Sharing it
is giving voice
to our mutual grief.

It hurts sometimes,
just to survive.

Until flight
breaks the bonds

that have frozen you,
please sing your pain
for all to hear.

The birds at dawn in springtime
sing their most joyful music,
and flight is a recourse
taken only by the brave.

Join that choir.
Loosen the bonds that impede
and fly to your destiny.

In the fields of your dreams,
there are still many songs to be sung.
There lies
your perfect
winged
fortune.

Beneath the Sky

Your soul
finds sanctuary
in pure emptiness.

Part of you
can always dwell there,
being at once
both within
and beyond
this world of light and dark conveyances.

The door is always open.

Motion, you ask?

Our essential best friend.

Walk the path.

The heart ceaselessly pulses
thru life's journey.
All those muscles lift you
into each day.
Necessity brings its own rewards.

But sometimes, you must carry more weight

than just your own bag
of flesh and bones.

When you see someone who is broken,
pick them up and carry them.
Give your body to others
as someone once
did for you.

It is true:
Your heart
needs wings
to dispel
all the misleading stories
from beneath the sky.

A Seeker's Elegy

I went to the well
to drink pure cool water,
and to nourish
my strength
from within.

In this becoming,
some infinite turning,
again
my heart
did renew.

I returned to the well,
in silence unbounded,
where grace
brought peace
to my soul.

Now here in this yearning,
as liquid as life,
freedom
brings courage
untold.

For the First Time

These things I hold dear

the sky
tiered clouds
buoyant
below unending cerulean
adrift
like giant boats
suspended
in slow motion unison
moving eastward
under curfew
from no-one

trees of a dozen greens
and more still to come
another season
shows its true colors

the iris and columbine
holding first blooms
flamboyant
yet quiet in their splendor

bright orange poppies
fresh as the day they were born
which was today

in fields of green grasses
luxurious with new growth
long and swaying
like tresses in May breezes
moving in unison
seeming to laugh
with reckless passion
and care freedom
for existence

for the first time
secure in their being
in ways we couldn't imagine
not long ago

it's a way of knowing
unique to this season
that goes on abundantly
renewed like flowers
for the alter
like a young child's eyes
just woken from a nap
looking expectantly
into this world
all trusting and refreshed
once again new
this too
for the first time

Summer Song

I think of you
in many ways
and at many times.
How could it be otherwise?
Especially,
I think of you on sunny days
of flower-lined garden paths
and the wild summer fields
in carefree profusion.
Colors,
the open sky,
are met by butterfly wings
and the happiness that insects
must know as they fly
single-minded
amid the riches
of pollen and nectar
drinking and eating their fill.
So that joyfully
simply
they may bring forward
this dance
once again
humming through it all.

Autumn

autumn
crept into the landscape today
warm toned trees
casting their brilliance
a flamboyant
short-lived undoing
colorful newcomers
after six months of green
held sway

in place of ease
grown to seem endless
in the fullness of August abundance
come newborn stirrings
gusts of cold
forgoing the last
of summer's bounty

discarding leaves
on the forest floor
all shades
eventually brown
down now for good

except for the tawny beeches
their flickering movements
shivering defiant whispers
to gravity and wind

fires start again
in contrast
to growing cold

harvest is over
but its' comforts endure

warmth comes
in nourishing food
the sharing of leisure
and the company of the familiar

I pull my coat closer
feeling change
is the currency of the day

winds come
from a new direction
the sky turns in different circles now
northern stars rule night
while summer's carefree sentinels
disappear over the horizon
and daylight plunges
diminishing
diminishing
until light
once again
return

Again Comes Winter

wild grasses
now straw colored, russet and brown
austere landscape's dried remnants
still colorful
going down to soil
or biding their time
until another season

open fields
graceful dusting of snow
dormancy has come to the land
poised for new beginnings
months from now
earth merely sleeps

rocks revealed
in woods newly bare
forest interiors
smelling of humus
sweet and earthy, oaken

something crisp and promising
woodsmoke in the air
throwing heat
into newly closeted places
a point of no return
winter isn't leaving anytime soon

it came in thru floors and windows first
seeping like cold
taking refuge from itself
filling all the spaces
shivering bodies
and woodstoves
couldn't reach
time to settle
away from winter's threatening bite
into late December comforts

snow, falling fast now
thickening as we speak
of soup, and good things to come
we rest and look inward
the short days
fading quickly like the light
into memories
of younger years
I too know retreat

the year closes
a new one beginning
days longer
ever so slowly
stretching wings
to begin again
chasing spring.

Ouroboros

Autumn is upon us now
and Summer's reign has passed,
receding into dwindling days
now rich with colors fast.

Which in their brief, flamboyant ends
do grant us bright reprise,
of many layered colors deep
within the green disguised.

This season is a wizened one
that brings its greens to gold,
and to the earth returns again
what limbs can no more hold.

For sure as Winter brings the cold
and with it rain and snow,
the fallen blanket rocks and roots
and become new soil below.

In the Spring new green we'll see,
nourished by last year's cast,
life renewed and led by light
into lengthening days at last.

My Other Half

For twelve long years
I've waited
for a love
that hasn't come.

"How long must this go on,"
I implored with frustration
to anyone who would listen.

"As long as it takes,"
I heard in reply.

Was it an old friend
imparting the wind
with empty words again?

I half think so.

But another voice inside me says
"This is only the beginning.
Every day is a new opportunity,"
and I cannot argue with that!

The empire of Summer is full,
but sometimes too hot to handle.

Autumn is fleeting,
one last brilliance
before the turning in
of Winter's austere darkness.

But give me one hundred Springs
and I will trade them all
for the other three.

My other half wants this
like there is no tomorrow.

The Water I Love

The water I love
buoys with ease
gravity's relentless pull.

The water I love
soothes me gently
when agitation preys on my will.

The water I love
warms me easily
when fiercest cold won't relent.

The water I love
shares without needing,
giving equally to every intent.

The water I love
brings balance to living,
transparent to all who'd deceive.

The water I love
flows where it needs to,
crossing hidden divides unseen.

The water | love
gives back to the earth
what was taken by hot, hungry winds.

And gives without question
in silent reserve
to balance what's essential to keep.

The water | love
brings with it ease
when work is left undone.

The water | love
gives back in good measure
greedy tribute taken by the sun.

The water | love
awakens with laughter,
when silence has little to tell.

The water | love
renews me endlessly,
when time's toll is taken all too well.

The water | love,
the water | love,
the water,
| love.

Temple of My Familiar

Like so many others, easily conceived,
into this world I was cast,
gathering gradually, gained at some cost,
bits and pieces of life I was passed.

Until I had gathered enough for myself,
basic truths I knew I believed,
and spun them into thread, in colors bold,
a tapestry now I would weave.

So I built the temple of my familiar,
of things that were always to last,
filling its walls and the spaces inside,
with stories and dreams from the past.

In this story-filled, unbounded space,
I dreamt again and again,
that the beautiful spirit of life as I wished,
was the sweetest balm for my pain.

Into these dreams I gave all my heart,
and guarded it well there inside,
in my temple, where no one could see,
except those who were also to abide.

This story was safe, a well with reserve,
so I trusted and bided my time,
keeping an eye, always the searcher,
open to what I could find.

But searching has limits, and I went about life,
and all its daily routines,
with the seasons as backdrop, an inconvenient truth,
soliloquy left me unseen.

To wait for epiphany is to wait in vain,
so into the world I was freed,
leaving the temple, now too familiar,
I planted a very different seed.

And for a time, to my fulfillment,
in work and in play I remained;
gained at more cost, time more measured,
youthful impulses more deeply restrained.

I gathered thru duty, and with it rewards,
in purpose I now did resolve,
and answered in turn, questions of meaning,
my soul urgently needing to evolve.

Until once again, work was fulfilled,
I found new questions arose

searching still farther, and deeper in Love,
my purpose now truly exposed.

To the temple I now returned,
to see and reflect on my path,
adjusting as needed, anew to my purpose,
replacing what had long since passed.

For all who share in the journey can find,
new tends replace the old,
and in the search for meaning,
some things are abandoned,
while others remain pure gold.

I reside, now, in my temple familiar,
where life's greater truths do dwell,
for love and wisdom, together in concert,
renew from a much deeper well.

So drink, you will find, with others in turn,
who seek and receive in due course,
their purpose, now greater, much like my own,
with Love as a limitless source.

In this temple of my familiar,
I will forever remain,
and gather together seekers in peace,
the balance I carefully sustain.

Peace

Snow falls
nearly silent
transient

countless
whispering
crystals

joyful
sky
music

moving
in
grace

gently
blanketing
the land

in peace.

I long for this moment
to continue
eternally.

Always

Yes, to the redbuds
enlivening Spring,
bright to bright,
life again sings.

And yes, to the sunshine,
golden and warm,
softening hardness
which long winters bring.

And again, to the lightness
gentle breezes stir,
inside all souls
which hunger for more.

All the full richness
this season renews,
for the faithful and enduring,
brightening anew.

Without A Mask

sweet ataraxia

almost nameless
like beginning a thought
when the quiet place
of your mind
has found home

a place apart
away
inside itself
grounded

we all rest

islands
of our own
anonymity

I thought
this concealment
would leave me
feeling muted
helpless
without a voice

when in fact
it's just the beginning
of something original

look inside and see
what a joy it is
to create
with no-one watching

Rise Again, Diamond Sun

This is the day you've always known.
It's completely yours.

To walk upright
on this good earth
the sun as your guide,
is like having some ancient friend
we all share.

In being here
to do our best,
we really need friends like that!

This warmth of our soft being
is to be freed.

Like water, like light,
communing with the brightness
and the shadows in turn,
us each being
vessels of our own everything.

The big hole that you once dug,
the dust of all those important things
that owned your spirit
and mortgaged it to ruthless bankers,
forget them,
lest they become traps
you never needed to fall into.

Rise

The rich wholeness of ten thousand days lived,
days of sorrow, of joy,
of returning curiosity:
We are imperfect carbon jewels of limitlessness.
Never forget that!

Rise again.

It's time to realize your fullest potential.
The occasion is now.

Blue fidelity, open sky,
Love is the sweetest nectar you'll ever need.
Become an expression
of all the lasting days
you've ever lived.

Rise again,
diamond sun.

Rise again,
your triumph is yours to own.

While We Walk This Earth

You said so little that I could not already see.
Redundancy. Old habits. Small talk.
There was a deep tiredness in that, and redundancy
behind your eyes.

You gave it a good face, but I could see through,
through to the more difficult place
that troubled you.
The weight of sorrow
pulling your mouth
down into a frown.

Very heavy.
What was there, I wondered?
I dared not ask.

We walked slowly,
trying to enjoy the moment,
on the way home from coffee,
thru the graveyard
where all was peaceful.

Restful, relax.
Tension, contract.
Hold, remember.
Ease, forget.

Stepping up the gentle incline
of a graveyard hill
with effort
you struggled with your cane.

I wanted to say, "rest now, don't worry."
But you exhibited a kind of weariness,
like being trapped inside of nothing new
for too long.

The pathos I could feel,
the sorrow that ran
into deep places
that few had access to.

There was some hope, though it was short lived,
like a pause is for gathering thoughts.
It faded, and the moment passed.

Rest.
There was a bench.
You must keep going
and you must rest, too.
Paradox.

Until you don't need to keep going, that is.
It's just peaceful then.
We looked around at the gravestones.

That topic was off limits,
almost unspeakable.
I certainly wasn't going to bring it up.

How could we talk of death,
especially on a day like today?

It was beautiful,
the crispness of the air
complemented the sun
so perfectly.

Cherry blossoms filled branches,
cast welcoming shade.
There was nothing to be down about, at all.
"Look closely" I said.
"Find something to enjoy in each day,
in each moment,
while we walk this earth."

"That's it. Exactly," you responded.
"While we walk this earth."

Your eyes lit up
with enthusiasm then,
a big smile came
and swept up

your entire face.

Now I could see that it all would be ok.
You knew yourself well.

Everything is perfect.
And imperfect.
That was a dualism I could embrace.

You knew that, too.
You knew so much.
There was little I could add
that offered you more.

One of the many gifts of age was knowledge.

I smiled, we walked on,
reassured that the day
and the season
were new.
This was all that was needed.

It was Spring,
and raining cherry blossoms again.
an ephemeral gift
that happens
on special days
like today.

On the Inside

Hearts,

easily broken,

mend slowly,

until the scars are borne

only on the inside.

Hide them, at least until the storm passes.

It's safest that way.

So it is with the flesh.

At first bearing scars without acceptance,

they too begin to blend

with greater ease.

They become bearable, less visible,

until time has done its work.

Looking beyond yourself,

resistance becomes reluctance,

becomes tempered willingness.

Finally, a little cautious optimism.

Nature takes its course gradually,

like rivers carve mountains,

like lifetimes spent wondering why.

There is meaning in suffering, but it's a

very different thing than finding love.

We all must try, but it's hard sometimes.

Meanwhile, scars are meant to be worn

without shame.

How are they healing?

How they're not.

How they, marks of survival,

are badges of courage

first placed there

to save you.

They hurt sometimes.

Carved into us intricately, crudely,

they simplify into an uneasy confederation

of good fortune and haplessness.

Invisible to those

who don't know where,

or care to look closely.

Invisible to those

who spare you the burden

of not seeing

what cannot help

but being seen.

Awake, keen eyes.

Soften now.

I'd rather sleep, dream the dreams

that speak to me

when wakefulness cannot.

Morning was unwelcome today.

Morning cannot give me back years lost.

Yet I took it, as I take almost all things,

in stride, forgiven

for starting without me

on the road home.

Murmuration's

On the edge of hope
there is a place of being
so unendingly stark
that desolation
has more meaning.

It is abandoned to all except me,
the heliopause of my existence.

Despair,
becoming emptiness itself,
brings the burden home only to me
when all else fails.

I wait patiently,
though trust can be hard to find.

Hiding,
something undeniably inward,
we function with few words,
for there is nothing to say
that has not already been said.

I disappear into myself,
letting wasted words fall away
into the silent recesses of my mind.

It is the lightness, bearable
and unbearable

on the dark side of hope,
when too few
ever take time
to understand.

                    Looking only inward
                        for fundamentals,
            away from all things superficial.

It is sleep, aloneness, darkness
that gives me a place to work
unhindered
until lightness
comes again.

                        It is very placid,
            and some lightening comes, eventually.

Breath and body lead the way.
The mind holds no new answers
and old ones are meaningless.

To escape this prison
is to find purpose again,
past the desolation and devastation
that dominates my being,
toward compassion,
to another season,
a season of hope.

Housekeeping At Dawn

Dream clouds
obscure distant horizons,
great currents intersecting in the sky.

At any distance, there is light.

Twinkling stars,
sultry moon,
heaven's azure lightness,
clouds floating
between stone and infinity.

This far from the sun,
water is always in motion.
Mixing, falling, flowing,
with stardust to the sea.

It covers the earth with prayers.

As water is for life,
my mind needs mesmerizing.

Time passing
brings inevitable change.

Diverse richness
is the universe in process.

We are everything we know,
and even death is only a kind of remaking.

Darkness is not for the frail or lighthearted -
this pain is the cost of being human.

So slow down, and know this:

It is you who must open the doors and windows daily,
to let the gravity inside,
then back out again
into the world.

73

Icarus' Lament

In the shadows
of growing twilight
I stand alone.

Natural as the sky, alive
within the great continuity,
yet among thorns,
I contemplate
a world to come.

Miraculously,
this earth has been my sanctuary.
Despite uncertainty,
all I have ever needed
has been close
or within reach.

But now,
the shape of change,
like some ultimatum, looms.

Inescapable,
above and below,
eclipsed by extremes,
torn by divergent strains,
there is no place to hide.

Rooted long ago
in everything youthful,
dignity now resigns
to better days,
and casts its lessons
to hot, dry winds.

In its place,
quickening toward morning,
a reckoning awaits
of far greater amplitude
than any we've ever known.

The past recedes
we can only move forward
into some uncertain dawn
in the shadows
of the rising sun.

Soliloquy Of the Soul

Just one week of winter
visited this year.
I can't remember now
when it's been
so succinctly brief.

Don't tell me you are not awake,
not aware of the change.

It's so obvious, isn't it?
The time to act, so short.

What am I doing,
plunging toward the unknown
without an exit plan?

There is no escape anyway.

Dwelling in vulnerability,
the restless stirrings
of a warming planet

quicken,

while I wring my hands

with worry.

I cannot sleep.

I want to scream.

Close your eyes if you must,

but only for a short while.

I will sound the alarm.

Now!

A mirror needs light

like a heart needs its mind.

I have my soul.

But does humanity have one,

even when all together,

under one sun?

I think not.

What morning can you rise

that is not at least

some small seed of opportunity?

There is still time to act.

After all, becoming something new

often requires

letting go

of other things.

How can I build a bridge to where you are,

awake in the darkness,

wanting to turn back

to yesterday

once again?

Yesterday is gone.

When children of all colors

have only today

to save what remains

of a diminishing world,

who is to blame?

Always A Cost

What Has Been Lost:

Clarity,
        skies without the artificial
        masking in monochrome
        and monotone artificiality.

        Instead, their night offerings
        countless galaxies
        and stars of lucent
        diaphanous beauty...

Water,
        untainted by anything foreign
        it's purity testamentary
        to things most valued by men
        in the long run.

        Pristine ecosystems,
        sustained and resilient,
        with plenty for us,
        leaving plenty
        for those who follow...

Earth,
>   intoning countless songs,
>   voices of the many
>   who don't need to own
>   to feel at home.

>   Unique.
>   Wildly diverse.
>   Irreplaceable.
>   Balanced.

>   But far too few believe.
>   Man plays such an eminent part
>   in extinction...

Ethics,
>   often under informed
>   by conscience
>   or consequence,
>   left out of the picture
>   far too often.

>   The bottom line
>   takes precedence
>   once again,
>   over all.
>   Count them down.

The evolutionary clock
subtracts faster now...

Wilderness,
for its own sake
becomes a fragile thing
under human toil.

Too fragile to lose altogether,
yet somehow,
too easy to disregard
and damage
until unrecognizable.

Where does responsibility begin
when pieces of a global puzzle
disappear.

In their place
nothing
betrays the silence?

Omissions,
while distractions
fill the void
to oblivion's
darkest hour.

The Best Compass

Time passes slowly
when you are but one small, new being,
filled with possibility.

It is in us from the beginning.
Children at play
live closer to the truth
than all the conquering armies
of human exploit.

After the rain,
watching twilight fade
into night again,
I pause, and remember:

Don't let the great window
of your night sky
fade into nothing;

Open your mind to everything.
Dream in moons,
and awaken

in the balm

of so many suns.

Yet sometimes,

there are far too many faces

of the unkind here.

We forget,

and in forgetting,

must catch ourselves

before we fall any further.

We can get lost without even knowing,

how far we've been pulled down

until we see no light, nor hope.

Yet even the darkest of nights

still contain light.

Remember to look up.

Clouds of many colors,

like ever moving storytellers,

or journeymen messengers,

remind us of the safest shores.

The Great Wheel

Summer is growing old.
I taste the dust in the air,
and witness the fading
where once all was new.

The changes have begun.

Leaves of muted vitality,
harbingers stir memories,
and whisper of the new spectacle
soon to come.

When you show your full colors,
Oh, I will rejoice!

I need the forests,
as I am of them,
and they are in me.

Oh, Great Mother, I am a weeping child.
Our separation creates yearning.
In my heart there is need for your embrace.
Together in this realm of light and dark,
the Great Wheel is turning.

The Teacher

Sky opens to everything.
Gravity is best thought of as a friend.
The moon moves far more
than the vastness of the sea.
And there are truths greater
than earth can hold in its irresistible, fluid embrace.

Winter deepens into cold truth,
teaching me to look closer.
I am stilled.
Summer fills me with light,
and all my oldest and best friends
are there in my heart.
Each time
Spring and Autumn
again display their splendor,
that same splendor
I've known more years than I can count,
I am still in love.

Some days,
I feel that, outside of the sky,
I do not know a thing.
This is good,
for it is an invitation.

On others, I think I know everything,
but reality spoils the party.
This I accept, until the stillness returns.
When all is clear, that is best.

How narrow
must our thinking become
before we give up in confusion?

Perhaps mystery is greatness
simply disguising itself
in the cloak of earth's green goodness?

Perhaps its rationality
wearing a cloak of many colors.
We all want to be dazzled!

But certainly, it is a gift,
knowing this steadfast pageant
for so many days.

Chance
and good fortune
have given you a variety of things.
Canvas. Circumstance. Timing.

And now too much pain?

There are stories there,
if anyone will listen.
Life's not a path
which all follow to the same songs.

You must know more
than thought alone can lead to.
But I am no fool.

Pure rationality has its place,
until your luck runs out,
and you are cornered
not understanding love
in all its splendid colors.

There are bridges still to cross,
dark waters suddenly
where once there was only reflection and light.
When all these inescapable truths
become something we cannot turn away from
lest we suffer too much,
we most need the sincerest of friends,
the best of strengths,
on our journey to safety.
Be light for some other's darkness.
When you can feel true joy at their successes,
it's like a door opening
to realms where few boundaries exist.

A Potter's Testimony

Cicadas sing their long summer song,
to a dry grass season
of hot sun
and shortening days.

August is fully upon us.

Fingers work sticky earth
into the possibility of treasure.

From toils in sweat,
smoke and ash;
born of fire
the crucible, brick,

our creative urges
forge lasting offerings,
fused
and frozen in time.

Mystics Recourse

wind brings uncertain promise
until it too turns
into something completely different
it's that way when it's angry
as trust can last a lifetime
or be gone in a moment's breath
the wind can be like that

but tonight, all is still
the cool spring air
quietly settling
into night
on open ground
close as their breath

far away
on an opposing mountain
another distant fire
remotely glimmering
offers a reminder
that they are not alone

bellies full and spirits warm
shadows huddling them closer
the ancients settle around a fire
that has burned for hours

adding wood
sparks trace comforting trails
up out into the night
merging before going out
to countless stars in a darkened sky
converting matter
to warmth and light
as they fly

a man gazes upward
stirring the fire
with a stick
that doubles as a cane
sparks fly again

all places have stars, he considers
hanging in the air so far overhead
they move around us
at different speeds
fascinating
some are bigger than others
hmmm

and the moon
circling around
how is that possible?
what holds it up?
and what is it made of?

how long have we been watching this way?
a long time, he concludes
a very long time
we go back forever

what is this world?
a wonder, he concedes
there is no other explanation
so many questions
so vast it's bewildering
marvelous and fascinating

his thoughts merge with the sky above
sparks flying higher now
eyes following them upward
into the sky

the others are gazing upward, too
quietly considering this place, this world
his thoughts merge with theirs
and then with the sky above

the sparks are gone now
the fire turned inwards
settling to coals
he feels small
but in a good way

91

contentment fills him

how is it that we die
when we live again through our children?

we live on in so many ways, he realizes
it is beautiful

the group fall victim to silence's trance
each with their own thoughts
taking in the stillness
of another night
in the open

for tonight
the questions outweigh the answers
all in good time, he thinks

the quiet sets in
as flames diminish
to a warming glow
the man smiles knowingly at himself
as the fire wanes
and they settle in for sleep
in an open land
in an open mind

Coming Home

In the soft glow
of afternoon sun,
on a westward street
I sit, gazing.

It is the end of April,
Springtime at its freshest,
full expression.

The mild temperature brings ease,
the longer days a brightness
worthy of basking.

The light, returning
growing in abundance
as with everything living
feels like a warm friend.

Slanting, long rays
welcome me home
after winters austere forbiddances.

The birds, too, rejoin the chorus,
trilling songs
to whomsoever will listen
as intently as they sing
rejoicing in being alive

without looking back.

What they have left
is all we have, too.

The chance
to live once more
in the open
without fear,
alive to all that is,
alive to all that will come.

Renewal

I fell back into myself today.

Happening suddenly,
it felt like an eternity
that I had been away.

Wandering, wondering,
desolate, hopeful,
facing winds of torment
and tempted by illusion,
with an eye on adventure,
and another
on hope

...always
wanting
home.

Every New Step

Journey,
journey,
journey,

until you surpass all weariness.

Every new step
will carry you
closer
to the sea.

Phoebe

Phoebe's emphatic voice
pierces night's greying vestige.

Awake at dawn,
a new season begins.

Bridge of Light

There is a bridge of light

between your eyes.

From its center,

a smiling fisherman

dangles

a silent,

golden

thread,

down

into the center

of your chest,

to show you the way.

Dreaming Wide Awake

After too many days
peopled by the mundane,
I have no idea
how just one day
suddenly can become
singularly fascinating.

Like a fast-moving boat
engaged by the wind,
full of new friends,
it's all excitement.

Awake again,
now finding myself alive
in all my senses.

Joy in just being
amid the chaos and the flurry
of a rapidly shifting scene.

A bright smile bursts from my heart
celebrating all the color
of a crowded night carnival.

Each Fleeting Moment

Every anomaly,
each fleeting moment,
what else
can I do
but smile
at life
another time...

...and remember
to ask knowingly
without a trace of regret :

Can
this
magnificence
truly
be
real ?!!

Opening

I glory in,
and surrender to,
the beauty,
grace,
and awe,
of life's unfolding dance.

And take refuge in the stillness
that comes when I am whole
within the infinite space
of the quiet,
loving mind.

Afterward

Writing poems is the start of a book. There's editing before submitting to publishers, where much additional editing takes place. Cover design, formatting, printing, promotion, marketing.

Special thanks to Don Gallegher for help with preliminary suggestions, as well as Nick Ramone, Jazz and the team at KDP Books. I appreciate your patience with my lack of acumen where you are expert. It seems that the process will never end, and then, voila, there is a book to share.

And funding - $2,500 from contributors who helped to fund part of the cost of publishing. Your generosity in this endeavor my first journey into published poetry a waking dream.

Heartfelt thanks to my saving angels Kay Schultz and Sheryl Strasser. The aid and assistance you provided me during my long illness came through in big ways that were irreplaceable.

And to Harry Lewis, Kay Smith, Ann Miles, Doc McCluskey, Jane Strasser, Scarlet Fannin, Rose Sincevich, Susan Frey, Fred and Andi, Rodrigo Tarraza, Megan Kealy, and others. You provided me with food, rides, housing, and/or moral support in my many hours of need. It made a difference where a difference was needed. I will try to pay it forward in some way. Thank you, thank you, thank you.

Rebecca Winder Oliver

In Memory of a soul
who succumbed to cancer too soon.
What a life well lived.

About the Author

Robert Strasser prefers never to be too far from nature if he can help it. Whether gardening with native plants, studying wild flowers, exploring hidden and out of the way places. His steps take him off the beaten track.

Wild places and natural processes have always held a fascination for him, which are explored principally through studio ceramics. Specializing in slip decoration, natural impression tiles, hand drum making, and spherical sculptures, working in clay is a lifelong passion. He went twice to Japan, in 2000 and 2002, for a cultural exchange and a residency in ceramic arts. He enjoys music, reading history, and hiking when he has time.

Balancing the arts, he worked as a wilderness camp counselor and staff, property manager, middle school teacher, and as a chestnut restoration biologist for 4.5 years. He has a BA in Biology and an MS in Environmental Biology from Earlham and Hood Colleges, respectively. He lives and works in Frederick, Maryland and Shepherdstown, West Virginia. This is his first book of poems.

www.ingramcontent.com/pod-product-compliance
Lightning Source LLC
Chambersburg PA
CBHW050256151225
36791CB00035B/203